BLACK-FOOTED FERRET

Black-footed Ferret

DENISE CASEY

Photographs by

DR. TIM W. CLARK

Dodd, Mead & Company : New York

A SKYLIGHT BOOK

Frontispiece: *Sunrise finds this ferret still aboveground. Ferrets are primarily nocturnal.*

Distributed in Canada by
McClelland and Stewart Limited, Toronto
Printed in Hong Kong by South China Printing Company

1 2 3 4 5 6 7 8 9 10

Library of Congress Cataloging in Publication Data

Casey, Denise.
  Black-footed ferret.

  (A Skylight book)
  Includes index.
  Summary: Describes the physical characteristics,
habits, life cycle, history, and future prospects of the
small animal that may be the rarest mammal in North
America.
  1. Black-footed ferret—Juvenile literature.
[1. Black-footed ferret. 2. Ferrets] I. Clark, Tim W.,
ill. II. Title.
QL737.C25C38 1985   599.74′447   85-4505
ISBN 0-396-08625-X

FOR TIM

C   5

ACKNOWLEDGMENTS

Many thanks to Lucille Hogg and Betty Thomas for encouraging me to write this book; Marcia Casey, Helen Ballew, and Rosanne M. Lauer for many useful suggestions; and the many Meeteetse, Wyoming, ranchers and citizens who cooperated with our research. Our efforts have been supported and funded by the Wildlife Preservation Trust International, New York Zoological Society's Animal Research and Conservation Center, World Wildlife Fund-U.S., National Geographic Society, Charles A. Lindbergh Fund, The Nature Conservancy, Joseph Henry Fund of the National Academy of Sciences, Defenders of Wildlife, National Wildlife Federation, Humane Society of the United States, Chicago Zoological Society, Fremont County (Wyoming) Audubon Club, Murie Audubon Club (Casper, Wyoming), and the Bethesda-Chevy Chase Chapter of the Izaak Walton League of America. Our research has been conducted in cooperation with the U.S. Fish and Wildlife Service, Wyoming Game and Fish Department, and Wyoming Bureau of Land Management.

Contents

A ferret's eyes brilliantly reflect light from a researcher's spotlight. Thomas
M. Campbell III

1
First Sighting

It was on a lucky St. Patrick's Day that I saw my first black-footed ferret. The other researchers and I were bumping across the dark prairie in trucks equipped with spotlights when we spied two emerald-green eyes reflecting our light. Although we had searched many prairie dog colonies for years for this rare and elusive weasel-like animal, this broad plain at the base of the Absaroka Mountains in Wyoming was the first place they had been found in almost ten years. I stood in the snow watching the ferret in wonder. Could this quick, lively animal, so curious yet watchful, be one of the last members of a species so rare that it is in danger of becoming extinct?

11

Ferrets are so rare because their main prey, prairie dogs, has been widely destroyed. For almost a hundred years, most ranchers and farmers have feared that prairie dogs competed with their cattle for grass and that their colonies occupied land where crops could be planted. To

A family of prairie dogs at their burrow. The ferret's chief prey, prairie dogs are highly social squirrel-like animals which live in underground burrows.

provide more land for cattle and crops, ranchers spread poisoned grain over millions of acres.of prairie dog colonies. When the prairie dogs ate the poisoned grain, they died, and many whole colonies were destroyed. Scientists say that in many areas the number of prairie dogs has been reduced by 95 percent since the beginning of this century. The ferrets, which depend on the prairie dogs for food, may eat the poisoned dead prairie dogs and die also. But worse, there are simply fewer prairie dogs across the countryside for them to eat and fewer burrows for them to live in. In addition, it's too far between remaining colonies for the young ferrets to disperse, and the few ferrets that are left are spread out in colonies too far apart to find each other to mate. It is a tragedy that this unique predator is the victim of man's widespread destruction of prairie dogs.

I was fortunate to be one of the very few wildlife biologists to study the little-known ferret. Sponsored by Wildlife Preservation Trust International, New York Zoological Society, National Geographic Society, World Wildlife Fund-US, and other conservation groups, our

The author trains her binoculars on a ferret and records its behavior at close range.

research team worked toward two goals: *conservation*, or protecting the small group of ferrets in Wyoming, and *recovery*, or helping the species increase its numbers until it can sustain itself. We had to answer many questions: How many ferrets are there and how well are they doing? What are the immediate threats to them and their habitat, or the place where they live? Are more young born here every year than this habitat can support? Do any undis-

14

covered ferrets still exist in other areas? How can we build their numbers and protect them?

This mysterious creature had baffled science for a long time. Dr. Tim W. Clark, who headed our research team, had looked for ferrets in Wyoming since 1973. His search included educating people about the seldom-seen ferret, inviting them to report any sightings of ferrets, and spending many weeks each year looking for ferrets himself. He didn't get discouraged, even though no ferrets were found in the state until eight years later. We have cooperated with ranchers, the U.S. Fish and Wildlife Service, Wyoming Game and Fish Department, Wyoming Bureau of Land Management, and other concerned groups in gathering data and planning to save the Wyoming ferrets. We realized that we had to "ferret out" this animal's secrets and unlock the keys to its survival. Our studies would have to continue for several years until the questions were answered and the species was recovered. We were encouraged by people from across the country who supported our work and who valued America's wildlife.

Black-footed ferrets are most often seen at the entrances of prairie dog burrows.

2
Masked Bandit of the Prairies

The black-footed ferret (*Mustela nigripes*) may be the rarest mammal in North America. Some even thought it was extinct until the population in Wyoming was discovered.

Black-footed ferrets are members of a mammal group known as mustelids, or weasel-like animals. Mustelids range in size from the least weasel, which weighs barely one to two ounces, to the sea otter, which may tip the scales at a hefty one hundred pounds. Mustelids have longish bodies and short legs, well-developed claws, short, rounded ears, and scent glands under the tail. Their robust skulls and strong jaws and teeth, including large

17

Often all that is seen of a ferret is its head in a burrow. This one is attended by a large fly on its head.

canine teeth, are adapted for meat eating. Sixty-four species of mustelids live in different parts of the world (except Australia, Antarctica, and most oceanic islands). Few people are familiar with North America's only ferret, although many of its mustelid relatives are well known. Everyone loves the mink's soft fur and the otter's playfulness, but gives plenty of room to black-and-white skunks and burly badgers. Porcupine-eating fishers and bearlike wolverines are scarce today, as are the lovely orange-throated martens. The three North American species of small darting weasels are fairly common, but one must be quick to catch a glimpse of them.

Black-footed ferrets are difficult to study. As they evolved over the eons, they became more and more specialized in hunting prairie dogs, and now they spend most of their time underground in prairie dog burrows. (They probably don't dig their own burrows.) Here they sleep, hide their food, escape from predators and harsh weather, and give birth to their young. Most active at night, they come aboveground for only very short periods to hunt and find new burrows or mates. Because they have adapted to this secretive kind of life, it is a challenge to fi id them and learn what they are doing.

A ferret is about eighteen to twenty inches l ng, including a five-inch tail. It weighs only one-and-a-half to two-and-a-half pounds. Males are somewhat larger than females. Although a ferret may spend many minutes motionless, peering from a burrow opening with just its head showing, it is nearly always on the move when aboveground. It bounds in springy, graceful leaps through the grass from burrow to burrow. Sometimes it stands up thin and tall on its hind legs looking and sniffing—for food or danger or perhaps a mate.

The black-footed ferret is well adapted to its prairie environment. Its color and markings blend so well with the soil and plants that one can hardly detect it until it moves. This slender, wiry animal has a black face mask, black feet, and a black-tipped tail. The rest of its short, sleek fur is a yellow-buff color which is lighter on the belly and nearly white on the forehead, muzzle, and throat. A ferret's coat does not turn white in winter as a weasel's coat does. When it raises up its muscular neck in an alert

20

Standing on its hind legs allows an alert ferret to see and smell more of its environment.

stance, one can see its short legs with front paws and claws developed for digging. Its large ears and eyes suggest it has acute hearing and sight, but smell is probably its most important sense for hunting prey underground in the dark. Although ferrets in captivity have reached twelve years of age, they probably only live to five or six years in the wild.

This species, native to North America, is quite different from the fitch ferret sold in pet stores sometimes under the name "black-footed ferret." The fitch ferret has been domesticated since the fourth century B.C. and was used by the ancient Persians, Greeks, and Romans to hunt rabbits. It has a dark mask and dark feet, but it is a plumper animal than the American ferret and its fur is longer, darker, and coarser. Also, its entire tail is black, while the true black-footed ferret's tail is black only at the tip. Our ferret is an endangered species and protected by state and federal governments, so no black-footed ferrets can be sold in pet stores. None has been kept in zoos since the early 1900s.

Its long slender body allows the black-footed ferret to move easily in underground tunnels.

3
History of the
Black-footed Ferret

The ferret's closest relatives are the steppe polecat in Asia and the European polecat. The dark brown European polecat lives in open forests and meadows, eats small mammals, frogs, and fish, and makes dens in crevices, hollow logs, or other animals' burrows. It is thought to be the ancestor of the domesticated fitch ferret. The steppe polecat looks almost identical to the black-footed ferret and leads a similar life on open grasslands and semideserts across the entire length of Russia. It hunts ground squirrels and lives in their burrows. Because it preys on pikas, marmots, hamsters, and other rodents, farmers like the steppe polecat.

Scientists believe that ancestors of the steppe polecats migrated across the land bridge which existed between Siberia and Alaska many tens of thousands of years ago. As these polecats moved onto the Great Plains, their

Laboratory studies on the steppe polecat from Russia have contributed much to our understanding of ferret nutrition and energy requirements.

behavior gradually changed until they were hunting mainly prairie dogs. Over thousands of years of coevolution with their new prairie dog prey, their biology and behavior gradually changed to suit this new environment. Thus, they evolved into today's black-footed ferrets.

Pispiza etopta sapa, meaning "black-faced prairie dog," is the Sioux Indian name for the black-footed ferret. The Pawnees called it the "ground dog." The Indians knew of the close association between prairie dogs and ferrets, which have lived together for many thousands of years. Ferret and prairie dog skeletons have been found in camps occupied by prehistoric Indians.

Various Indian tribes had different beliefs about ferrets and used them in different ways. Some captured and ate them. In some Pawnee stories, black-footed ferrets had special powers. The Cheyenne and Blackfeet decorated chiefs' headdresses with their furs. The Crow used them for sacred ceremonies of the Tobacco Societies or for medicine bundles. A few of these ferret skins, stuffed with cotton and decorated with colored cloth, leather, bells, and feathers, can now be seen in museums.

It seems almost as if the mysterious ferret has been hiding behind its mask. None of the early explorers, mountain men, or wagon-train pioneers who crossed the Great Plains ever mentioned ferrets, although many remarked that prairie dogs were everywhere. Although some ferret skins were shipped during the fur trade, the ferret

Three medicine bundles made of stuffed black-footed ferret skins by Crow Indians about 1870, now in the Chief Plenty Coups Museum in Pryor, Montana.

was not recognized by scientists until 1851 in a book by John James Audubon, the famous naturalist and artist, and the Reverend John Bachman. And they had seen only one specimen! Because no other ferrets were reported again for over twenty years, some scientists thought these authors had invented this strange mustelid to put in their book. Throughout the years, however, a few ranchers and sportsmen reported seeing ferrets. Some even kept them as pets and learned about their behavior.

Although ferrets were rarely seen, biologists today believe that they did not actually become rare until after the widespread destruction of prairie dog colonies. These poisoning efforts began before the turn of the century and continue today, but were heaviest during the 1910s through the 1930s. It was not until the 1960s that people tried to save ferrets from extinction. By this time, it was almost too late. A few ferrets were found and studied in South Dakota, but then they too mysteriously disappeared. For years, only scattered reports were made. Then finally in 1981, the small population in Wyoming was discovered.

4
Studying a Rare Mammal

Because black-footed ferrets are nocturnal, ground-dwelling, secretive, and solitary, they have remained a riddle. How many people spend their nights wide awake on prairie dog colonies—when even the prairie dogs are asleep—just to have a chance of finding ferrets?

Biologists have devised many methods of studying ferrets despite their elusive ways. We drive through the colonies at night shining spotlights over the ground to locate and count ferrets and observe their behavior. The ferret's eyes reflect these spotlights with a bright green color, just as a rabbit's or deer's eyes shine in the headlights of a car.

Another way to learn about them is to hunt for the signs they leave, such as tracks in the snow. Tracking is true sleuth's work. We follow their footprints step by step, investigating where they hunted and measuring how far they bounded through the snow looking and sniffing in one prairie dog burrow after another. Occasionally, we find marks in the snow which show that a ferret captured a prairie dog and dragged it to another burrow.

Another sign we seek is the unique diggings ferrets make by dragging dirt out of prairie dog burrows and stringing it out in a long thin pile on the surface. We measured one dirt heap 11½ feet long. Another ferret we snowtracked made four diggings in one night and dragged a total of ninety pounds of dirt to the surface! We have examined the diggings closely, but we haven't unearthed any clues about why they dig. Is it to get at prairie dogs to eat? To hollow out a space to sleep or hide in? There are so many questions.

Signs of the elusive ferret. Black-footed ferret tracks (crossed by tiny mouse tracks) lead to a prairie dog burrow, where the ferret dug dirt out of the burrow. The ferret then left, dragging a prairie dog away.

Left: *Researcher Louise Richardson examines a digging made earlier by a ferret. Since no other animals on prairie dog colonies make diggings of this size and shape, this sign gives us a clue that ferrets are present.* Below: *By catching ferrets in specially designed traps, researchers can examine them without handling them. The men are wearing face masks to avoid contaminating the ferrets.*

We also study ferrets indirectly by examining the prairie dog colony itself to see if it differs from colonies where ferrets do not live. We study the prairie dogs, the plants, the other animals that live there, and the human uses of the land, too. This can help us understand the ferrets' needs for food and shelter.

Laboratory tests on the closely related steppe polecat give us a good idea of the ferret's nutritional needs and energy uses. Computer models of ferret genetics, predator-prey relationships, and population sizes and space needs are useful. With these, we can begin to understand complex biological systems, evaluate the health of the Wyoming population, and set goals for future research toward eventual recovery of the species.

5
Life in the Prairie Dog Colonies

Much of the central United States consists of vast rolling prairies of short- and medium-length grasses. In the western parts, sweet-smelling sagebrush grows. It is here on the Great Plains that prairie dogs live in social groups called "colonies." One can see the low mounds of dirt around their burrow openings on many hundreds of acres of the Great Plains. During the day, these squirrel-like rodents nibble grasses and weeds, groom each other, or gather grasses for nests—and always keep alert for predators. They chatter to each other constantly, and one can hear their "yip-yip" from far away.

Although black-footed ferrets have occasionally been

Above: *A black-footed ferret in its natural prairie habitat. Prairie dog colonies which have harbored ferrets range from very dry to quite lush. Here grasses, sagebrush, and other shrubs grow.* Right: *One of the prairie dog's chief occupations is eating. They must store enough fat to survive the lean winters when little or no food is available.*

found living in haystacks, around buildings and towns, or in ground squirrel colonies, their main natural habitat is prairie dog colonies. Biologists believe that ferrets once lived in all the same regions where prairie dogs were found—from southern Alberta and Saskatchewan in Canada south to Texas, New Mexico, and Arizona.

The wide prairies may seem barren and lonely to someone who is used to trees, hills, and lakes, or to someone

who is used to busy city life. But in fact, prairie dog colonies are rich communities of many species bound together in a web of relationships. Each species has its own design for living and its own role in its community. Once huge herds of bison roamed the prairies and wallowed in the dust on prairie dog colonies. Pronghorns

Bison have always been at home on prairie dog colonies.

Pronghorns graze at the base of the mountains.

still browse the sagebrush there, their white rump patches flashing when they sprint from dangers. Elk often graze the prairies near the mountains where they can escape the summer heat. At dawn in May, male sage grouse strut in their spectacular courtship displays. In June, rainstorms come rumbling after each other out of the mountains, and the air is alive with the songs of mea-

Male sage grouse in their springtime courtship display. They strut before the females, puff up air sacs in their chests, and make a curious, deep, bubbling sound.

dowlarks, sparrows, and blackbirds. Around the marshes and small creeks lined by cottonwoods, many species of shorebirds and wading birds make their home, and fields of wild irises paint the prairies soft blue.

Coyotes, foxes, skunks, badgers, and weasels hunt in prairie dog colonies, as do some snakes and many birds of prey, such as hawks, eagles, falcons, and owls. Once, wolves and grizzly bears also prowled there. Besides

Above: *A prairie hunter, the coyote, may take ferrets as well as many other small mammals and birds.* Right: *A large prairie dog mound like this may have several burrow openings. Here a ferret digs at one of them.*

hunting the prairie dogs, these predators catch and eat ground squirrels, gophers, mice, rabbits, birds, and insects.

A prairie dog burrow is a good place for ferrets to live. It stays cool through the hot, dry summers and warm in winter. Most tunnels have small rooms off to the side where the ferrets can build nests. Some have two or more entrances so they can escape if chased. Many small prairie animals use prairie dog burrows for these reasons.

6
Mothers
and Young

Each ferret seems to have a separate area where it hunts throughout the winter, and from this we conclude that ferrets spend most of their lives alone, not living in groups. But in mid-March, their tracks begin to overlap as if they were becoming more sociable. From this, we assume that the mating season has begun. We have learned that after females and males mate they do not stay together as some animals do, nor do the males help in raising the young.

The litters of one to five ferret kits are born in May or June in prairie dog burrows, although we haven't discovered how the females prepare the nests. At birth, the tiny ferret kits' eyes are shut tightly, and their fur has

44

no markings. Their only food is their mother's milk. The mothers are so secretive that sometimes we can't even tell which burrows the kits are in. Occasionally, the mothers carry the kits by the back of the neck to new burrows, as cats move their kittens. The babies don't venture aboveground until they are several weeks old.

By mid-July, the kits are about half grown and able to come aboveground by themselves. Their eyes are open now, and their fur has the same markings as their mother's. We watch as a mother leaves a burrow in the quiet of the night and checks the safety of the area by looking and sniffing the air for several minutes. She looks in nearby burrows to make sure there are no dangers. Then she returns to her babies and coaxes them to follow her. If they are shy and scared, she pulls them by the neck. As they grow older and more confident, they follow readily when she calls to them. Sometimes they move a few feet but then scurry back to the safety of the old burrow. But finally they all bound after her in single file through the grass. Together, they look like a toy train, each little ferret closely following the one ahead of it, their eyes

A mother ferret tugs her reluctant youngster out of a burrow by the ear.

shining like headlights in the reflection of our spotlight.
Sometimes the mother leads them to a burrow where she
has left a dead prairie dog, for they have started to eat
meat by now. Other times, she leaves her offspring in a
burrow, then hunts and brings prairie dogs back to them.

46

The ferret kits grow very fast. By late summer, they are nearly full grown. They come aboveground at night and during the mornings to play around their burrows. They jump at each other and dance and hop backward. They arch their backs and tails, walk on their tiptoes, and flip over. They nip each other's ears and noses. One man who raised a young ferret long ago said it liked to sneak up and grab a person's cuff or heel! They chase flies and chase each other in and out of burrows. Like

Three young ferrets (one hiding low in the grass) watch for the return of their mother.

A hawk consumes a prairie dog. Hawks often hunt on prairie dog colonies, where they may catch ferrets as well as other small animals.

puppies, they turn in circles to bite their tails. When their mother approaches, she is greeted with playful jumps and bites, too. Our studies show that the family stays together through the summer. The kits spend nearly all their time in the burrow where their mother leaves them. Long after they stop nursing, they depend on her for meals of meat. Although they appear full grown and some weigh more than their mothers, they are not very adventuresome and do not know how to hunt successfully by themselves.

But the instinct to hunt is very powerful, and they learn quickly. It's amusing to watch them try at first to "hunt" rocks, flowers, or other things. They crouch and stare at flowers, creep toward them, and pounce quickly. Soon they are stalking grasshoppers and larks and mice. They practice over and over, because it is a kind of game for them. Their skills and confidence improve with this practice, and eventually they learn to hunt prairie dogs successfully.

They must learn other important skills, too, like watching for dangers. We once saw a hawk fly over a colony

A researcher's spotlight catches a young ferret in the pre-dawn hours.

and swoop down on two ferret kits playing on a burrow mound. It was a great relief to us when the kits saw the hawk just in time and dove into the burrow. Young ferrets need to be on guard against other predators, too, such as the powerful badger, which can tunnel into the burrows after them.

By late summer, we observe that the mothers leave their kits in separate burrows during the day. They still bring them food at first and gather them together at night to hunt. But eventually, the young begin to hunt for themselves by night and sleep alone in the day. After a while, the family no longer lives together at all. The young ferrets become independent and solitary, and in the fall, some of them leave the area where they were born to go to other prairie dog colonies.

However, in this region of Wyoming, there are few prairie dog colonies near their birthplace. In olden days, there were many large prairie dog colonies, especially on the grasslands bordering rivers and streams. Dispersing ferrets could easily find new colonies by heading in almost any direction. Now, however, ferrets are much less likely to find new colonies, even by staying near the waterways. Once the young leave their home colony, there may be no prairie dogs for them to eat, and they must find other less suitable food and perhaps compete with other animals for it. Without the safety of prairie dog burrows to hide and sleep in, they are vulnerable to predators and accidents.

Our spotlighting in October reveals fewer ferrets after the young have left. I often wonder how many have made it safely to new prairie dog colonies.

This mother ferret will take the prairie dog she has caught to feed her four youngsters.

7
Hunting

Just after dawn one morning, a prairie dog poked its head aboveground. Dr. Clark watched as a mother ferret jumped at the back of its head so hard that they both tumbled back into the burrow. A moment later, she reappeared, looked around cautiously, dragged the dead prairie dog to a nearby burrow, and dropped it inside. She kept watching and dragging the dead prairie dog from burrow to burrow until she brought it to the burrow with her young inside. Ferrets rarely attack prairie dogs aboveground, and Dr. Clark was very lucky to witness this hunt.

Ferrets occasionally hunt mice, ground squirrels, gophers, or small rabbits. People have seen them eat birds, lizards, eggs, and insects such as moths, grasshoppers, and flies. But although these other foods supplement their diet, black-footed ferrets are extremely dependent on prairie dogs for their overall survival. Since prairie dogs live in groups, it appears that the ferret usually has a ready supply of food. Even though some prairie dogs hibernate, or go into a special kind of deep sleep in the winter, ferrets can dig them out.

We watched a mother ferret digging in a burrow one night. She backed out again and again with dirt held against her chest with her front paws. Each time she dragged the dirt a little farther, sometimes kicking it backward. The pile of dirt she left was about six inches wide and eight feet long with a trough down the center where her body had smoothed the dirt. Then she quickly descended and brought up three dead young prairie dogs. She carried them one by one in her mouth to a new burrow. Leaving them there, she joined her own babies. The next night, she moved her kits to the burrow with the dead prairie dogs in it. They remained there for three days to eat them. This observation excited us because

A ferret has taken a large prairie dog.

we learned how ferrets hunt and choose small prey, how they dig, store food, and provide for their young. By giving us a clear picture of their needs and behaviors, this kind of information will be valuable in planning ways to save them.

The ferret has different strategies, or plans, for hunting. Of course, the most common is hunting at night when the prairie dogs are asleep in their burrows. This gives the ferret an advantage over the prairie dogs, which may be as big or bigger than the ferret. If the ferret hunts aboveground, it tries to pull the prairie dog down a burrow even though the prairie dog struggles and braces its feet against the entrance. If a ferret leaps on a prairie dog's back, the prairie dog rolls over and fights with sharp teeth and claws. It's very risky for ferrets to hunt prairie dogs.

Mother ferrets often have large wounds and scars on their faces and necks. We suspect most of these injuries are the result of battles with prairie dogs. The mother ferrets may be injured so often, since they must find and kill a lot of prairie dogs to feed their growing youngsters. By the time the young start to hunt for themselves, the

Researchers think this female's wounds resulted from attacking prairie dogs for food for herself and her young.

mothers are thin and their coats worn from their hard work.

Black feet and black masks give black-footed ferrets a striking and elegant appearance.

8
Hope for the Future

What will happen to this mustelid behind the mask, a symbol of the mystery and enchantment of nature? Since we were responsible for causing the ferret's rare and endangered status, we must be responsible for trying to save them now that that opportunity exists. The web of life in which we all share will remain strong and whole only if we exercise a wise stewardship of nature.

New human activities now endanger the ferret, too. There is much exploration and drilling for oil and natural gas in many areas of the West. Vast coal fields will be dug soon to provide energy for our country. Many of these human activities will destroy prairie dog colonies, leaving less and less habitat for ferrets and the other animals that depend on prairie dog colonies for food and shelter.

Because the ferret population is so low and because there are so many threats to them, biologists and conservationists fear that the black-footed ferret may not survive without our help. Many conservation groups, universities, private citizens, concerned scientists, and government agencies are joining together to protect the ferrets in Wyoming and to try to find them in other remote regions where prairie dogs still live.

This is another part of the detective story. Just as there are many ways to learn about ferrets, there are many approaches to saving them. Everyone agrees that the goal is to increase their numbers and to ensure that they have safe places to live. Some scientists have followed dispersing animals very closely to learn what happens to them. By documenting their behaviors and habits, we can best learn of their needs. We are also perfecting ways of locating ferrets so we can find them if any exist in new areas.

Some endangered species are bred in captivity so that the young can be safely raised to maturity and then released into the wild. Members of some species are captured and released into other safe habitats. These two recovery techniques may be used with ferrets. Special preserves may be set aside for them. Ranchers, oil companies, land management agencies, and all other users of the land are encouraged to use the land wisely to avoid harming ferrets.

Many other animals worldwide share the endangered fate of the black-footed ferret. Many scientists have devoted long years to finding out how best to help these endangered and rare species. Only with dedication and cooperation can we give these animals the chance to live naturally in their wild state. Only when ferrets are restored to a healthy status will we all have a chance to glimpse the mysterious "masked bandit" of the prairies.

Index